DEAR MOM, DEAR SON

SEPARATED BY BARS NOT THE HEART

D1417360

BY

LINDA L RUTHERFORD & JASON JD RUTHERFORD

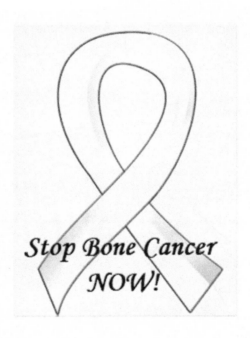

ISBN: 9781981060726

ISBN-13: 978-1981060726

ACKNOWLEDGMENTS

A big thanks to all those who stuck by my side while I was behind bars. THAT MEANS YOU MOM!

Thank you, Thomas Quintana, Chris Jaquez, Rick Durfey, Jan Stuck (RIP), Leann Tucker, and Dr. Herlickson for teaching me the tools of life I failed to learn. Big thanks to all my new-found friends and acquaintances who have proven to be true friends. Big thanks to all of you mothers out there who I have met affected by the incarceration madness; Terri Robinson, Sue Cody, Angela Monshower-Hernandez, Jamie Belcher, Davene Ingram, and all the rest of you that struggles with the separation by bars, but not the heart

A huge thanks to all those same people from my mother.

DEDICATION

This book is dedicated to my beautiful mother.

Linda Lee Rutherford

December 26, 1948- June 20, 2016.

Even though you are gone from this world, your spirit lives on in
my heart and on the pages of this book. I love you, Momma. I'm
living each day keeping the promise I made to you.

Introduction

The beauty of writing and the power it holds is magical on many levels. Put into music or poetry, it becomes a life form with the ability to affect the reader and listener alike. Poetry is more than the artistic expression of thoughts, feelings, and ideas. It is thoughts, feelings, and ideas of a spiritual nature. The tongue of the soul or so to speak where the hand is nothing more than the courier.

Poetry has been used in everything from the star-spangled banner to hip hop. Even ancient historical text like the Epic of Gilgamesh and the Enuma Elish are counted amongst the oldest known poetic creations while the Book of Psalms, although consider religious, demonstrates a poetic struggle of the human heart.

Poetry is written and heard differently by everyone. Since there are so many variations demonstrates the vast creative universe for which words originate from. For me, it is my soul singing to the world a variety of songs that expresses my true inner self. While we communicate through the vibrations of our voice box, poetry communicates through the harmonics of something far more divine and esoteric. Maybe that is why it moves so many to tears of joy thus affecting the listener's spirit in a powerful way. Yes, words are powerful! Poetry takes the ability to speak and turns every word into a separate journey as the word's own emotion.

I must count myself extremely blessed to be able to understand this art. Yet it is not just me alone. Artistic talent is something that runs deep in my blood. Far back in the gene pool from generations past, there have been artists of all kinds. Builders, painters, writers, sculptors, musicians, and, of course, poets. I do believe that I inherited my poetic talent from my mother of which brings us to this very special book.

When it came to the many different forms of poetic expression, my mother owned nearly every one of them winning first place time and time again in online poetry guilds. She was a truly gifted writer who sought to express how she saw the world through the lens of her own mind. In the poetic arts, I learned a great deal from her and went on to create many works of emotion expressed with ink and paper myself.

I was once asked if the student could outshine the master? I never saw my work as being anything close to the level her art was at. Nevertheless, I hung on and shared my work with her, even occasionally, online in her poetry circles. I saw firsthand in these circles just how superior her skills were. Nevertheless, she remained humble, teaching me that one cannot truly say that this poet is better than the other. All have their own distinct kind of beauty; like a tropical island compared to a majestic mountainside.

My interest in her writing came at an early age. I still remember way back when I was a small child. I used to listen to the poems that she would read me. Beautiful pieces of work like: "Soldier Boy" and "Lucifer." There were many others, but those ones always stood out the most. It was like music. Fine music that spoke to my soul. It was a calling! A calling from a power higher above than myself telling me that the ability is also within my own heart. I would go for several more years before I knew that I also possessed this beautiful gift. The ability to flow rhythmically is not hard if you really put your mind to it. I knew I could do it if I put forth all the energy I possessed inside myself.

It came to me one afternoon while I was on the phone with this girl that I had met at Knott's Berry Farm, in Buena Park California. Just like a typical teenage boy, I did everything that I could to court her attention. I remember reading a couple of my mother's poems to her as if they were my own. She became so impressed and intrigued that she asked me to write her a poem.

Chills went down my spine! What the hell was I going to do? I never wrote poetry before! Hell! I could barely even write a letter. I wasn't exactly a stellar student in school. So, what to do? I hung

7

up the phone with her and I sat down to write. I had writer's block before I even knew it. I tried to ask my mother to help me, but she refused. Instead, she told me If she could write poetry, I could as well. I picked my brain finding no help there. I then looked into my heart and just like that, the words magically started to flow right out onto the paper as the ink formed letters across the college rule piece of paper:

THIS PAIN I FEEL

Your voice is warm and so sincere;

are you far away or near?

This pain I feel is sad and real;

to hear your voice, makes my heart heal.

I know we've only talked a few short times;

but maybe someday you will be mine.

Love has hurt you, so it's love you fear;

but girl I hope you know I'm here.

If you were mine I would treat you right;

fall in love with you I might.

I know others hurt, cheat, and lie;

they do not care if they make you cry.

But one comes along who's true and real;

and he's the one that will end the pain you feel.

June 1991.

And there it was. Just like that, my poetry was born. I cannot even begin to describe to you exactly what kind of feedback I got from her, it is not appropriate for this book. The point being, since that time, I was writing. I mostly dabbled around with writing rap lyrics. I would sometimes entertain others with the street influenced poetic rhymes that expressed what I was feeling inside. As a troubled at-risk youth who believed that the streets were his home, I used poetry to vent; to protest in rebellious fashion putting the world on notice. I even wrote a suicide poem once when I believed that life was not worth living. It's strange how a lot of poets share this obsession with dark matters, I mean, look at Edgar Allan Poe. Judging by how influential rap music became shows just how many others also share an affinity with this dark art. Like anything, this music evolved into something far removed from where it came from or did it? Again, there is no orthodox system for poetry.

Then there was my lyrics. Now I know I never hit it big like Dr. Dre, or Eminem, but that did not stop me from dabbling in my own expression of the art itself. Most of my lyrics were started up the traditional way of any other rap song of the day; coming straight out, busting a cap in that ass with, or without a beat:

Busting wicked rhymes called the criminal flow;

J.D. straight macken o.g. money making pro.

Putting in a gang of work so I can get rich;

and I don't have time for this stupid little bitch.

Pretty ridiculous and crude, to use one's gift in this fashion, is what my mother believed. She never viewed rap lyrics as poetry or art for that matter. To this day I would have to disagree with her. Rap music was a new form of poetry joining the others as another addition to the catalog.

So, it did not stop there. In one ear and out the other. I turned up the volume even louder in the words of everything I did in my daily life of crime.

Now I don't hit bitches;

I hit switches;

I hit snitches and I don't shit britches.

Now I ain't nothing nice;

I'm cold as ice;

I shake dice and I don't like mice.

Or:

I gotta stay strong, gotta push on;

and all these haters and hoes trying to do me wrong.

Ain't no love or no loyalty so what can I do;

if I get stressed out before you know it, I'm through.

Apocalyptic revelations are the signs of the times;

mental stocking my rhymes;

soaking bodies in limes;

staying ahead of these haters as they droppin their dimes;

so, I grab another pen and scribble out more lines.

I used to believe that people couldn't understand the mind of a rebellious child unless of course, you relate in some way by sharing the same struggle. It would make me laugh to hear how many people would bump Tupac, Biggie, NWA, or Snoop Dogg while never for one minute running the streets or busting a lick (crime). How can you relate to any of the words that the artist is speaking? That is what poetry is; A relation from one's emotion to another- an empathy! Shared between two or many. Without a common relationship in the struggle of the street thug, hoodlum, gangster; all one can lend is a sympathetic ear to the message in those lyrics. In this thinking, I was wrong. I failed to consider the imaginative spirit. The fantasy. Everyone is a gangsta to a certain degree in life, right? I mean one can hear busting caps in dat ass and picture a cap getting busted in the form of making that big sale at work or even drifting off to an alternate reality where they are a Tony Montana of sorts. Whatever it is, it's not for me to understand.

Being that someone's individual imagination is outside the scope of my understanding, who am I to say how anyone was feeling when they were hearing Lil Wayne? As an artist, I paint the picture according to how my soul is experiencing and feeling what is being colored. You the reader will empathize or sympathize with the words in relation or understanding forming your own mental picture that triggers the emotion. One can see the artist as just lashing out, trying to make a statement; just looking for attention. That is what poetry is all about, lashing out drawing attention-MAKING A STATEMENT!

Indeed, poetry is a means of seeking attention or to make a statement. So why would I be any different in making my own statement? My mother made several statements in what she was experiencing with her poetry, and often it was so esoteric that you could read beautiful verses without fully understanding what she was saying. No different than Capote or Poe, right? Exactly. Some poetry is so obvious while others, well! It's up to you to decide.

Here is obvious poetry in the words of my mother back in 2014 when we decided to write this book together. She published this poem for several hundred people to see all except one... Me! I recently found it online with many poems she wrote of which I've never gotten to enjoy until now. Maybe it was never meant to see, but upon discovery, I cannot even describe to you how it made me feel. Just listen to the emotion in her short words and you will understand completely what this book is all about and why it was so important for us to write it together.

A Troubled Son

A child grows, but not the way you hoped

both strong-willed and wayward thinking

a troubled teen and young manhood

lead to a troubled life

drugs and a jail cell

anger and doubt

never heard.

that screams

pain.

It took me several minutes to regain my composure after reading it myself. I mean, WOW! How powerful were those short verses in explaining just how my life choices had affected her? How she was totally in the dark as to the why and what a paradigm shift it was for her to get the full story from her son the exact nature of his pain. It opens up doors and visions of things never imagined or being totally unaware of their existence.

What she was saying is, over all the years of watching her son grow into a man, she saw this darkness within him and could not understand as to why he was hurting so bad. Oh, how helpless she felt in watching her only son destroy himself with drugs, gangs, and crime. A jail cell was the permanent home for her little boy where his anger and doubt journeyed to new heights. She never heard what he was saying. she was deaf to the screams of pain because he was so distant to her. The distance is what brought her all the pain she felt more so than the self-destruction.

You see how beautifully crafted her words are? A true gift that is intimidating like a giant who stands over you with its shadow completely covering you.

Then I read this one called monsters. It was hard to figure out just who or what she was talking about in this poem. To the ear, it sounds as if she was talking about politicians but the closer I read, I learned the exact nature of what it was all about.

Monsters
Shadows held within his hand,
loose to creep across the land.
Evil now each shadow hold,

with a dark and chilling cold.

The night it seems is finally here,

forever bringing with it fear.

To strike the heart and souls of men,

who traffic in the worst of sin.

And bring to each an early death,

set there by the devil's breath.

Probably one of her last writings as it was dated 2016; the year of her death. To me this poem, "Monsters" speaks volumes of emotion, being that I knew what she was going through. She knew death was looming closer. Not long before my mother passed, I confessed to her about some very horrific stuff that happened to me when I was a fourteen-year-old boy. I had experienced some real deal abuse at the hands of evil men who trafficked in child abuse in order to entertain a world of twisted sub-humans who got off on human exploitation. When she heard every gruesome detail, I could feel just how appalled she was. The numb silence on the other end of that phone told it all. I could hear her breathing, but that was all. Finally, she returned with questions, not for me, but for them. Just how could these men harm her little boy? And how much has karma settled the score? She believed that the devil does not come to harm the innocent, but the guilty. As a non-believer in religion, she saw this devil's breath as a sort of reaping what you sow. Hearing the fate of one of these pieces of garbage gave her a sense of peace in knowing that the others more than likely have faced a similar fate, for their shadows are held in his hand meaning; you can run but you can't hide, and your sin is never forgotten.

These works are touching for me. They give me so much appreciation for the woman who gave me life and the magic of writing. The ability to create a world of words manifests real effects from the words themselves. Like spells cast by a magician, or witch, woe to all who are the topic of the reaper poem, the one whose breath is the wind of retribution come upon you to bring your reward for the evil you do. Yes, deep within, she understood the power poems held. And as a mother whose heart was broke from news held secret for so long, I could only imagine what that poem might have done to who it was intended to affect.

The relationship my mother and I had was a distant one for so long. I have spent the better part of my life behind bars for a wide range of crimes ranging from drugs, guns, stolen property, gang-related crimes, and finally, to Federal Bank Robbery. Throughout the years, I never once tried to use my writing for something good. I spent time dabbling in fictional writing and started to write a book detailing a dramatic childhood but never really sat down and tried to put forth the effort in creating something that would last for all times and impact so many people that are experiencing these same issues.

When you have millions of people incarcerated in this country, I think it is safe to say that somewhere in this vast tomb of locked away souls, there is at least one mother standing by her son or daughter as they correspond together through bars all the emotions they are experiencing as a result of the sad situation and circumstances they are under. Most of these letters do not try to lecture or belittle, although at times they do get heated.

No, most communications that the incarcerated share with their loved ones is a sense of escape. A momentary sense of freedom as the familiar voice over the phone, or on paper, share with them what has happened since they were gone and what the future possibly holds.

I've experienced this for years. I kept close contact with my family through numerous prison terms in the California Prison System all the way up to my father's death. Once in Federal Prison, it was my mother who I kept close contact with. The moment we first talked about writing this book, we had to first reflect back to what we were feeling and how all this had affected us.

Before she even knew my thoughts, I quizzed her for the whole 15-minute phone call and even had to call back to finish hearing all the details of her struggle. All the pain and suffering I put her through. I listened to the exact nature of her broken heart spill out its experiences of the past in real time. It was very emotional and revealing. I knew at that moment that this book had to be written. There had to be something I could do to form a bond with my her. Like helping her cut potatoes, or tending a small garden out back; I saw this book as a way to reunite with a mother from the lost years of staying behind bars raised by the state system. Never once did we think we should send this to a publisher. It was for us to bond more than anything else and to share with generations to come.

However, my mother had mentioned a few times that this book could benefit others because, at the time, we had no plans of selling it. But I could see how every other mother and her son or daughter in prison could relate to this since the experience is the same and their own personal struggle is poetry in itself bringing to light the emotion and void while also inspiring hope that change can come to the ones that stand up and recognize just how difficult the whole experience is for both of them. I kept my promise to her by finishing this book and here it is.

Please excuse any mistakes in this book. I work two jobs, and go to full-time school; while also volunteering in the community when I can; and of course, getting this book to print. I did it all alone after my mother's death with no agents, editors, or proofreaders. I did it with love and honor, so what if it isn't perfect. This whole journey was far from perfect.

With that said, it is our pleasure to present to you our combined efforts in describing to you, in rhythmic expression, the exact nature of our relationship through bars and how hope never truly dies; for a mother always clings onto hope while also feeling the doubt ever haunting in the shadows waiting to disappoint once again. I hope that you can relate to this journey. I pray that you will create a bond with each other once again as my mother and I had done. With that bound, you can finally escape incarceration as your remorse guides you down the right path of freedom and happiness.

Dear Mom;

Once again cold prison bars separate me from you,

the world; from even myself, I think.

I know that others doubt the truth of my sincerity,

they doubt my goals- my dreams for prosperity.

How can I blame them for a pessimistic loss of hope?

when it was I who braided my own rope;

for I could not live without money and dope.

Trapped in a personal hell, selfish, lost and afraid,

oh, how many sleepless nights have I prayed.

That I would change for good and make you proud,

bring joy to your heart, always be around.

But just like so many times before I made a mistake,

playing games with my life with careless chances I take.

Risking death, meaning my last breath!

I don't think I have too many of them left.

So, I need to slow down, reevaluate my life,

never can give up, is the essence of my strife.

Though true, I know I said it all before,

that I will try to change and break laws no more.

One can sound like a record that's broke,

taking life for granted, like it was a joke.

Let my words be actions, and results you'll see,

it's all I can do for you to see the change in me.

Love;

Your Son

Dear Son;

Through all the years I've loved you and hope that you would see,

the crooked path that you followed could never set you free.

And there were times when I despaired that you would never learn,

that faith and peace within the soul is something you must earn.

It took so long for you to get to where you are today,

faith that lives within your heart that Peace that you display.

So many dreams were shattered so many tears I cried,

now all those dreams live again, and all my tears have dried.

Now you know prison life that's made of iron bars,

it can never harm your soul within as faith can leave no scars.

I know there are things within your past you wish you could forget,

for all they ever brought was pain and choices you regret.

26

But your faith has found a purpose that lights the path

ahead,

and the past is but an echo of things now long since

dead.

With love;

Mom

The Son

You would think that I made a thousand promises and broke every one of them. "I will change and break laws no more." The truth of the matter was, that my mother knew well, I never promised I would change. All I ever said was I will try, and as we all know trying don't cut it. Throughout my criminal life that's all I could afford; a good try! A simple crack at it while remaining pessimistic the whole time. The minute the shit hit the fan, I would throw in the towel and the rest is history, right back to the streets running with the homies, drugs, and crime.

However, listening to my mother's words, you can hear that glimmer of hope that must have clung on for dear life all these years. Like a beacon of hope, there was a voice in the back of her mind that said; 'He will change! He will change!!' once she read that first letter, all the dreams she had started to manifest as a possible reality.

Is it too late for a lifelong criminal to turn over a new leaf and live a straight life? according to my mother, no. According to everyone else, not a chance in hell. Who could blame the Nay Sayers? I mean after all. I will try to change, and break laws no more always sounded like, "I promise to change and break laws no more." Everyone in your family goes along for the prison ride one way or another. Everyone is doing the time with you, and for that, the resentment sets in deep and may never come out. A pessimistic loss of hope is a hard thing to overcome when you have watched someone you love destroy themselves over and over again.

Risking death repetitiously is the purest definition of insanity. Doing the same thing repeatedly; how many breaths of life could I possibly have left? The destructive behavior, criminal in nature, runs on a whole other level of energy that has baffled psychologists for decades. Many have tried to map this destructive level through theory, lobotomies, and of course, prison. "Playing games with my life with the careless chance I take," is classic. Oh, how many bandits in gunfighter lore have played this Russian Roulette with their lives? In these modern times, many of us stuck in the prison revolving door are no different in this respect.

And how about that deep inner insight she gave me? "Now you know a prison life that's made of iron bars, it can never harm your soul within as faith can leave no scars?" Strange passage, as faith does not possess the ability to scar. It is a moving force that drives the will. What she was trying to say is that faith must never waiver. No matter how many times you fail, it is the failure that scars if you allow it to live as self-fulfilling prophecy not the faith to carry on for it cannot scar.

The mother closes her eyes and pictures all the wonder and joy her child shows in the infancy of life. the sky is the limit for the child's innocence knows no corruption of soul or character. This hope of a bright future becomes a visual fantasy. The child who grows up to be president, or a doctor, lawyer; anything except the criminal he became. What a disappointment it is! All the heartache and pain that follows crushed dreams. The mother can only stand by as a spectator to the destruction.

Reading her words helped me open my eyes to this reality. How could I have put her through so much? Was I oblivious to this heartbreak I caused? Or was I simply blinded to the reality by a jaded sense of pride that carried me into the arms of the destructive devil I ran to time and time again? The right thing for me to do was assure her that I hear her. At this point, the only alternative was to let her know that I hear her.

Just want to let you know, Momma. I hear you. I really hear you! I'm sorry I cannot heal the wounds, but my actions sure can.

The Mother

How can I even describe to you how it feels for a mother to watch her child destroy himself? My heart had broken so many times I often wondered if I even had any heart left. Hope had always been there, I guess, but the doubt was always stronger. The cold prison bars he wrote about is more metaphorical to me. I mean, for many years there had been cold prison bars that separated us. They weren't physical, more like something I couldn't understand. There was a deep dark hurt possessing him. When I looked into his eyes I could see it, feel it! A mother knows when her child hurts. He is a part of me after all. What I don't think he understands is that when he goes away, I feel some sense of relief because I feel he is safer in prison than in the streets.

There were many nights I would pray, please God don't let me get that phone call no mother wants to get. Please don't let anything happen to my little boy. Because of this reoccurring nightmare, I would have to live over and over again, a personal loss of faith in a God died with every broken heart. I cried too many tears, and every night my mind was haunted from a side by side vision of when I wrapped Jason in a blanket as a baby, followed by placing him in a casket as a young man. It brings tears to my eyes to even confess this. I'm sorry but that is all I can say at this point.

I'm sorry ☹

Dear Mom;

I just read your letter; your words are very true,

how could I be so selfish for what I put you through?

All that pain!

All those tears!

Followed by the broken promises, throughout the years.

For the choice I made, took me down the wrong path,

taking everything for granted; Yielding karma's terrible

wrath.

You couldn't be more right regarding the faith I must

learn,

to put out this negative fire that deep within still burns.

But I will succeed I never felt like this before,

could it be that karma is done, has she finally settled the

score?

Like being born again, I truly found the way,

the straight path of the Essene brought me a better day.

And many more will come with this new faith I thought I

never had,

now I must learn to let it take me through good times as

well as all the bad.

Believing in myself is a hell of a fight with this pain deep

inside of me,

I awaken to this new realization that has really set me

free.

Love,

Your Son.

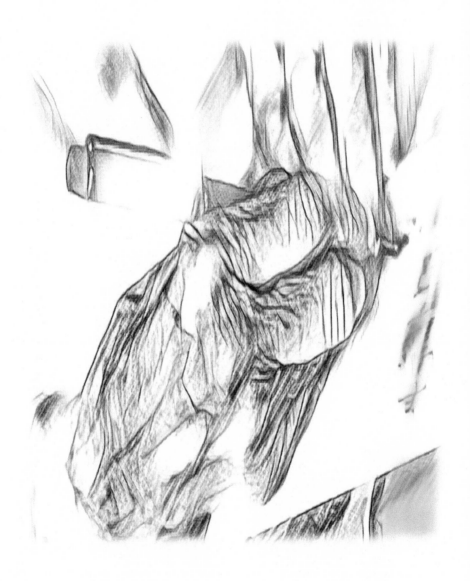

Dear Son;

Remember that a mother's heart is stronger than it

seems,

and all that it holds within is hope and heartfelt dreams.

Hope that you will find your way, dreams of your

success,

and find the life you should have had before your soul

transgressed.

Many times, I sadly Thought of things I could have

done,

to change all your yesterdays and change my only son.

But now I only look ahead to where your heart will lead,

and know the path you walk is proof that you'll succeed.

So, keep light within your soul, let it lead the way,

and know that you are in my heart and there you'll

always stay.

With love,

Mom

The Son

Choosing the path of an Essene is not an easy one. Especially since no one really has a clear idea as to what that path entails outside of speculation and personal spin. What it meant for me at the time was solitude and peace within the self. A complete turning the other cheek from all the destructive vices I had come to enjoy inside those walls. This would not be an easy task to separate me from the lifestyle inside the belly of the beast, yet not impossible if you really put your mind to it. So, I chose not to apologize for my conduct over the years, instead, I would show her with my actions. But how could she see what I was doing while inside? Good question and tuff to answer. The point was, it is the unseen effort that matters. As long as I know what it is, the rest will follow suit.

The fire within me still burnt hot. This demon of sorts that lived off the energy I fed with the evil deeds of my greed and chaotic personality I call Mr. Maddog. That crazy white Ese who had to go harder than the rest growing up in the California prison system constantly having to prove himself to his car he ran with. An endless test that any initiation hall of hell would have already completed long ago yet this one just seemed to go on and on forever.

My pride is what kept me engaged in these endless trials. NO LONGER!! Even if it meant my death or physical assault, I would stay the course and walk the walk of a true seeker of higher worlds enduring a whole another kind of suffrage and persecution; this time from my peers.

On my mother's end, it would seem that I was not giving her enough credit. While I was being underestimated, so was I underestimating her. Yes, your heart is stronger than it seems. It must be the hope and heartfelt dreams, after all! It is that faith we talked about before that is a powerful god force within the true adept that knows how to harness and control it.

Really, what could she have done differently to change it? "Many times, I sadly thought of things I could have done." To change all her yesterdays and change her only son." Yet change comes from a personal decision. A moral choice to finally return to rational thought and utilize simple coping mechanisms to overcome any situation before us. No, mom! There was nothing you could have done. But your endless love was enough to keep my heart beating. It was enough to finally see that if a mother would not give up on her son, then why should I give up on myself?

What a paradigm this was. The vision of a loving mother who holds her only son in her arms. She promises never to let him go even though his sins are weighing down one side of the scales.

Balance is restored with her words; "And know that you are in my heart and there you will always stay."

She stood by my side indeed. That was much more than I could say for my crew and my so-called homies that all but forgot me as I merely exist in this concrete tomb doing time. This fact cut deep, and I had to share it with her in my next letter.

The Mother

I often heard it said, that in a place like prison, men and women run to the churches and instantly become born again and set free by Jesus. I also heard, that many, once returned to society, forget the same Jesus that set them free.

It is hard for me to believe in a God that does not seem to possess any control or power over his creation. I think back to my personal experience with prayer. It was not enough to spare my father from Cancer that took his life. It was not enough to cure my husband of the nervous breakdown I watched him suffer as a result of his accident. It never prevented my son from himself. So how could there be any power in something so out of touch or control?

Yet here is my son now talking about the same things I heard about. It scares me to think that he could end up falling the same way so many others have; believing in some mythological figure to cling to in a time of turmoil and pain. I started to see religion as a security blanket, something to get one through the fear and uncertainty that prison obviously creates. Once the doors opened, the fear goes away, and they forget every word of every scripture.

However, this path he speaks of is not the usual Bible-thumping religious fervor you normally hear about. I gotta admit, what he's discovered was quite interesting. After all, I'm the one that does all his research for him. Countless hours of lookups he requests, and the copy and paste that I learned how to use through him. The books I've sent him, and the tone in his voice shows that whatever is working in him is something I can't explain, nor heard from him before.

I'm not ready to believe in a God just yet, but at least I can say something is happening inside the soul of my son, and I hope it continues. Then, of course, the reality is, he is confined from the world inside that prison. It's easy to say one thing while doing something totally different once released. Where he goes from here we will have to wait and see.

Dear Mom;

I thank the god within myself that your heart is strong,

how is it that so many others seem to have it wrong?

Locked away, far away in a cell I stay,

I watch the sunrise and set another day.

Where are all my friends, my peers, my homies on the

streets?

These are the thoughts I have at night as I lay between

the sheets.

Where are they, why does no one seem to care?

That I am trapped between these mountain peaks that is

the devil's lair.

I risked my life for others, my freedom just the same,

to have the back of so-called friends that play a Judas

game.

It's hard to trust, even harder to believe,

that there's some good left in this world that's made so

many grieve.

But I can't help but think, as cynical as it is,

we're born alone and die alone that's just the way it is.

Love;

Your Son

49

Dear Son;

We're not born alone, nor die alone, for your lord is
always there,
to help you over stony paths and heal your dark despair.
There are ones that care for us, but some will turn their
backs,
do not think the worst of them for feelings that they lack.
I know the life that you've led has made you how you
are,
it's hard to trust and believe in others when both can
leave a scar.
But do not let your anger live or have that final say,
or it will rule your very soul and lock your heart away.

With love;

Mom.

50

The Son

The sun rises, and it sets each and every day. Through the dirty glass and bars of my window, I can see the earth's shining source of power illuminate the day. It strolls the yard with us. It does not share the yard, for it is everywhere. It is not isolated to the yard for it moves from one end of the penitentiary to the next; jumping all fences of barbed wire and electricity. It is not a prisoner as I am, but it does not turn its back on me because I am in prison.

We all have peers on the streets. How many of them stay true and hold on once we are locked away? True they remain for a short period of time, yet over time they fade just like the sun does yet unlike the sun, they do not return until you are free then they shine once again. Not true for my mother. She rises and sets with the sun always returning the next day.

The reality of the mountain peaks deep in Colorado's Rocky Mountains is a valley stained with prisons. Broken dreams, and lost souls all around me. Most share this resentment for others they trusted, especially since in most cases those they trusted put them there. I too have my own personal Judas, and as I lay between the sheets it is hard to control those negative thoughts of retribution-Gangsta style!

"Do not think the worse of them for feelings that they lack," says my mother in her words of encouragement. Trust in others do leave scars, and the actions of a few can damage many future relationships. My mother tried to stress this point with the up-most importance. The anger that has the final say. The power to rule my decision-making process is not only a means to an end but imprisonment itself. It will rule your heart and lock your soul away. There is nothing worse than an incarcerated soul. Oh, how many people in this world are locked up in this way and do not even realize it? Screw that. I'm not gonna suffer double jeopardy! Not both body and soul locked up. My soul escapes this existence as I sleep. It is my escape from the reality that I am in.

Early in the morning, I'm on the yard. As I run the track in the thin mile high air, I watch the sun rise above my head as a reminder that I am alive and have so much to be thankful for. The will to survive and the ability to overcome the struggle lives within my heart. Those words my mother wrote have carved out the rot and void like cleaning out a pumpkin to plant a candle of light; the candle of light is my endurance.

As the weeks wound on, the Fourth Of July came. It was on that day I wrote what it really meant to me in the hopes that my mother would, in turn, share a thought on what she saw as a day of independence. While there were people attacking that holiday, I can't help but feel pity for them. The esoteric truth of that day is the freedom of the self from the world. The freedom to live and overcome no matter what others think of you. No matter whose thoughts are against you, it is we who control how we react to it. The Fourth Of July this year was a mark of my independence from my destructive self.

The Mother

Years slipped away from him. The time he did not only removed his body from society but his mind and understanding as well. All his nieces and nephews grew up until he couldn't recognize them anymore. His own mother grew older and older as well. His friends on the streets; his peers, either suffered the same fate as him, died, or moved on with their lives. But that's life, and that's the part of life I think he doesn't understand. I knew that he was captured for this bank robbery because of someone he thought he could trust turned him in. What did he expect? That is the lifestyle he chose. I know he expected one of his friends to go after the one that turned him in, but out of sight out of mind, and that is a part of life he also didn't learn. I remember that his dad use to tell him that in time after he spends years of his life in prison, his friends would show their true colors and move on. Well, Jason. What color are they? The only means of comfort I can give to mend his broken heart is advice. Yet, I can't help but think that maybe this lesson was healthy and necessary for his change. He needed to see through the lifestyle he held onto so tight for what it was; colorless and clear. Yes, your friends are showing you their true colors; transparent. So now you can see right through them.

Dear Mom;

When I close my eyes, I venture to another world where
all my fears turn to naught -slipping away like a thin wall of
mist that dissipates upon the rising sun,
my soul travels in this world where nothing matters
except the moment of joy and laughter; the bliss that is fun.
This is how I spend my life in a jail cell where my body
lies asleep in peace unaware,
completely unmoved and oblivious that the soul
experiences freedom only it can enjoy for a few short hours
outside of its lair.
I awoke today like any other day except today is the 4th
of July,
my mind wonders in remembrance of those nights
fireworks lit up the sky.
We all must choose a path to follow, the road beneath
our feet,
understanding must manifest itself with the trials we will
meet.
That is why I chose this day to mention memories of a
little boy who knew not the meaning of the 4th of July,

all he knew was wonderful fireworks so colorful that
burst up in the sky.

But I know now what I did not know the meaning of
things before,

that the struggle for independence deep within can be a
hard fought a war.

Like my soul that spreads its wings in freedom night
after night,

my body can be free from the tyranny that made the
dark turn to the light.

So, let this day be a day of independence from my
irrational negativity,

let me take on this world with the strength of a man you
said that I could be.

Love;

Your Son.

Dear Son;

In dreams, you could be everything you ever wanted to

be,

for they paint this world in colors that you want to see.

Bright with the promise of a better future, a better new

life,

free from all the worries of the past, free from all the

strife.

Where the problems that you see while awake seemed to

fade away,

replaced by the memories of that little boy on that

special day.

Keep goals and memories close to heart and let them

light the road,

and they will keep you on the right path and lighten up

your load.

For a man with a broken spirit is blind when life has hit

him on the chin,

and will walk the same broken path repeatedly to see

where he has been.

Walking down a better path is where he should go,

he must look deep inside himself to find his greatest foe.

Only then will he heal his spirit; find the strength to do

what's right,

know the path that he should walk and give him back his

sight.

All these things I've seen in you, of one lost who found

his way,

and all the pride I have in you is more than I can say.

With love;

Mom

The Son

How can one separate a dream from reality? Is there an unobtainable goal? The incarcerated constantly set the bar high often to an unrealistic height. This too I have done, for I am no different than the guy in the cell next to me. Yes, we may not share the same skin color or sit at the same table, but guess what? Both of us share the same struggle. Both our mothers share the same pain. We may try to kill each other out on that yard; stain the ground with each other's blood. But we cannot shank each other's dreams we have. No matter how high, dreams are the one thing no one can take or handcuff.

I chose the path I walked. Now on the day of independence, I can choose a new path. Dreams that I once believed were unobtainable are now a reality "We all must choose a path to follow, the road beneath our feet; understanding must manifest itself with the trials we will meet." The new path does not come paved, with street signs, and navigation. It comes as pure darkness.

This is the biggest roadblock of all. That blindness that turns to fear. None of us will admit to this fear. After all. We are the legend in our own minds. Quick to bust a cap to prove that fact. Quick to hide behind that mask the one I call; "Blue-Eyed Devil."

This devil was never my hopes and dreams. Yet it was my escape. My gateway drug, for the lifestyle was the most addictive influence in my life. Independence from the Blue-Eyed Devil was not gonna be an easy task, yet, like my mother said; "Keep goals and memories close to heart and let them light the road; And they will keep you on the right path and lighten up your load." The problem was, as I am making this transition, I left the goal part out since I could never seem to develop healthy goals, often setting unrealistic expectations and trying to pass them off as goals. Lightening my load meant I had to set realistic goals.

Where would I go to assist myself in this effort since all my best thinking got me stuck every single time? I decided to enroll in a cognitive behavioral therapy program to see if that could help set a fire under my ass. The model before me was designed to function as a substance abuse program. The problem with that is, I did not believe that drugs were my problem. The lifestyle was a real issue. I never broke the law to support my drug habit, but to support my criminal lifestyle as a whole. Yes, I struggled with the use of drugs, but generally speaking, my issues were much deeper. Admitting that I was a drug addict as a prerequisite to gain admittance was not a total lie. I saw my lifestyle as the drug, and the substances as the lighter, pipe, and needle to ingest, inhale, and shoot up; the lifestyle as a whole.

With an open mind, I am ready to take the next step in change. A process that is sure to be one of the most difficult challenges I have to face.

The Mother

I received a request from a counselor at the prison Jason is at asking me to write about how my son's incarceration has impacted my life. So here we go again. Since I already wrote about it here, I'm sure it's no secret to him now so the shock won't be as severe. Nevertheless, I did it anyway. I knew it was something that he would have to read before an audience, at least, that's what I hoped he would have to do.

Well, it turned out that he did have to read it to an audience. He wrote me back to tell me how it made him feel, and he said how much emotion he felt in that letter itself. I think what really opened his eyes was the fact that I stated that I no longer fear he will fail or return to his old ways. I see a tremendous change in him. I see it because I often see him in my dreams. It's silly to compare because dreams are not real, right? I can't really explain it to you because it's something only a mother can understand when experiencing this prison thing with her child. You honestly have to be in our shoes to understand it. We know when they are lying, and we know when something else is going on. I can sometimes feel the tension in his voice from the environment he lives in. It is like I am right there with him trapped in the cell as well.

So yes, I can honestly say, something good is happening to my child. Well Not a child anymore, because it seems like my son is finally growing up, and it looks like He is finally shaping into a man; one I knew he could always be.

Dear Mom;

Yes, it's true I found a way; a change that I have made,

for the very first time in my prison life, my twisted ways

now start to fade.

The tools I learned in a very short time exposed what I

think,

that irrational in nature are my thoughts in self-

destruction I did sink.

Roadblocks lined along my path, so I turned my back,

in a sea of pity, I chose, a spoon filled with dark death

smack.

Help comes knocking at your door from where you least

expect,

it is the one you thought the foe that shows what you

must correct.

Actively listening to what others say reveals an obvious

blind pain,

their constructive words will help me see why I must stay

in a single lane.

It still hurts my ears to hear what I would not see,

but my thoughts must be clear to what I hear for it will

set me free.

Jokes are made in negative minds so change they will

not find,

well, that's good for them but I will pass and leave this

prison life behind.

Love;

Your Son.

Dear Son;

This has been a time of growth, time to leave the past

behind,

let the truth you have found be the glue that holds the

strongest bind.

Walk the path that you found and take each step with pride,

even in the hardest times when all your dreams have died.

But with each setting sun, there comes a new day dawning

bright,

and better dreams to follow now a way to set things right.

Remember that a person's worth is always felt within,

and none may know another's heart or what their life has

been.

It's known the past can shape a man for better or for worse, but only you can make the choice between a blessing or a

curse.

So never judge yourself by what others think they may see,

for only you can know the truth of all that you may be.

With love;

Mom.

The Son

Resistance! Resistance at all cost! Yes, that is the little voice inside my head telling me, fuck these people. Upon entering this unit, I had all this hope believing that I would breeze through it. What little did I know is there was a force at work against me. A faction of assholes who sought to make my life miserable inside this program until I quit. I wasn't gonna let them win, and I wasn't gonna go away. I would stand and fight for this change process that needed to happen. There was too much at stake and too much for me to lose. My mother and I started this book project together and she had already received some heat from others on how I would not follow through, and how I would not change. I could do nothing to prove them wrong at this point. Right now, the truth of the matter is I did not possess the right mind set to release successfully. I am still fighting myself, and still allowing others to get into my head with the prison politics, and the CBT program politics-and, of course, there is that faction who stirs shit up on me!

"Walk the path that you have found and take each step with pride; For I know that it was hard when all your dreams have died." The pride she speaks of is not false pride, but the brand of pride that is driven by faith, and perseverance. The self-worth felt within is not something that needs to be on display as a simple showpiece. It is a character trait that goes without saying. self-worth is personal, and it does not involve anyone else.

The main point to everything I am doing is where do I see myself in five years. Am I locked in a cell? In the grave? Or could it be, that I find success in some unknown place of release? Will I find that special someone to fall in love with once again? A woman to share all my intimate secrets with? Share my life with, and live in that nice house I never thought I would see?

There is a lot of questions to be answered. I did want to be a family man, despite what others have told me regarding the spiritual path I chose; one that would complicate the family life. The further I got in my own esoteric studies of the occult, the more I am starting to see this idea as speculation, or opinion rather; one that was not rooted in the facts my soul was discovering each and every day.

"So never judge yourself by what others think they see." What one sees as a path for them, and all its components may not be the same for me. The most I could get out of this program was the ability to find my own path in life. I tried to follow the paths of others and failed. Yes, one should have a mentor or guru. But inevitably, one must be their own guru and the world their school. So, the help that came knocking at my door from who I least expect is all those who test me each day. Instead of allowing it to make me feel a certain way, I now have the ability to learn from each experience as tools to help me grow.

The Mother

Nobody ever said that change was easy, and I think Jason knows that now. I am so proud of him I can honestly say that now. I mean, every time he calls all he talks about is the process he is going through and all of his goals he is working on.

I know he has a spiritual mentor named Victor from the Essene Church of Peace in Maryland. It is one of the places I found for him when I was doing his research. Sometimes I get emails from Victor. This is how I know Jason is doing really good. Also, he sent us a video of him from one of the programs he completed in there, and the video was amazing. He talked about where he was at in his growth process. He was talking directly to me, and just being able to see his face eased any doubts I had about what my son was becoming.

I said I can feel it, Jason has changed look at him! His sisters doubt it. I try to advocate for him to no avail. I really can't blame them, I mean their doubt sometimes makes me think I might be naïve. But after that video, I know for a fact that he is different and when he gets out he's going to prove everyone wrong and I'm going to be right there every step of the way cheering him on.

I know this program is hard on him and others challenge him in all sorts of ways. All I can say is be patient. That is something he never had is patience. But now he is learning that the goals he is setting will not just come overnight, and this process as he keeps calling it will continue for the rest of his life. I love you, I am so very proud of you, and if I can say without hurting your feelings, it's the proudest I've ever been of you.

Dear Mom;

The road I walk can only be as hard as I allow it to be,

if I fail to learn the lessons that life gives to me.

I know I must let the past fade away and die,

Just like the clouds above that cover the bright blue sky.

For they grew dark with thunder, lightning, and rain,

kind of like our experiences that fill us with sadness,

sorrow, and pain.

Yet no storm is forever, one day they will pass,

that is how I see my past, its effects they cannot last.

It is my thoughts that fuel the fire that burns within my

mind,

I cannot move forward unless I choose to leave them all

behind.

Thank you for telling me, what I had to hear,

that my strength will weather all the hurt, that I no

longer fear.

One final thought I have before I mail this out,

beyond this world, we'll all move on, and that's what life's

about.

Your spirit will remain and mine will do the same,

and together in the cosmic realm above, we'll light the

eternal flame.

Love;

Your Son.

Dear Son;

Because you found the strength to leave all your fear

behind,

and look ahead without that fear of what you might

there find.

Know that I have seen it in dreams that I have had,

a future filled with promises, much more happy days

than sad.

I too have found the strength to walk a path I never

chose,

and just like you, without the fear of where this new

path goes.

It is my thoughts that fuel the fire that burns within my

mind,

I cannot move forward unless I choose to leave them all

behind.

So, do not much worry or fear for me, our strength will

see us through,

to a much happier time, where life can start anew.

And I know I'll be there to watch you take that first step,

into a new future, with all the promises that you and I

have kept.

With love;

Mom.

The Son

The image behind this poem shows what happens when I venture off the path. A return to that old lifestyle and all the bullshit is always one step behind me. It is like a Doberman Pincher just waiting to turn on me and bite. "I know I must let the past fade away and die," can only happen when I refuse to acknowledge the elephant in the room; that Blue-Eyed Devil behind me. "It is my thoughts that fuel the fire that burns within my mind; I cannot move forward unless I choose to leave them all behind."

Get Behind Me Devil! Blue-Eyed Devil, for he is a mutheafuckea! However, I am starting to see that he is only as powerful as I allow him to be. The eternal flame burns brighter than the dim flicker of the devil's candle. A flame of pure energy as opposed to a stick of wax. It is becoming easier to see these things the further I progress down this difficult road of change. To jump in the rabbit hole means to face all these fears with understanding as to what they're all about.

Then I read my mother's letter and start to feel like there is a much deeper esoteric layer to her words that I couldn't fully understand at the moment. My mind wanders, as I shift into the light of my meditation. I lose all my thoughts trapped in the material world and shift into the spiritual domain of the higher world that is consciousness. All the sadness and sorrow slip as I take a new breath. This is how I contemplate all the deep works of literature I read throughout the day. Now here I am on this astral plane examining these words of deep mystery.

"It is my thoughts that fuel the fire that burns within my mind;

I cannot move forward unless I choose to leave them all behind."

What is the true meaning of this passage? what has changed in her words? She has begun to talk about matters that are of the spiritual sense, but for what? My mother is a confessed atheist. When I asked her why she just simply stated, "how can a god exist in a world full of death, and destruction. Greed and corruption?" True. How can he? I tried to explain to her the reason for all of this according to what I have learned. But I didn't think that my answers were any more comforting to her since they are so far out of the mainstream schools of thought that incite anger in most because of the fear of what one does not understand. Instead of fear, for her, it is simply a turning away from it.

But then there was this verse;

"I too have found the strength to walk a path I never chose,

and just like you, without the fear of where this new path goes."

What is this path? And where does it go? I was caught up in this to the point of pure frustration. Death, a path, a life to start anew. These things spelled some dramatic shift. A change in life, some kind of event that I was having trouble understanding.

as I awoke to the reality of my cell once more, the meditation had ended. I decided to write her a letter detailing just exactly how I was feeling about this and to seek answers to some of my questions if of course there were answers to be had.

I sat down and started to write. My curiosity and confusion drove the will. My words flowed like the fresh waters of a river rolling downstream.

It is not hard to figure out just exactly what direction I am going to take this. The best way to proceed is to just let the spirit of my words guide me. Let them guide me down that stream. Let the wind fill my sails and push me towards that island of understanding.

I said;

Dear Mom;

*I have to say that for days now past my mind has spun in
doubt,*

*trying to pick apart your words and wonder what they're
all about.*

What is all this talk of death, and birth that starts anew?

*No matter how many times I read, I still don't have a
clue.*

*Maybe you are speaking metaphorically, for a lesson in
life I must learn,*

*but I can't help to feel this way, my thoughts of such
concern.*

*For the son can feel his mother's heart and know that
something weighs,*

*oh, what a minute! Let me backtrack my words, allow me
to rephrase.*

*Since you gave me life I feel your soul embracing me
each day,*

*a presence that surrounds my being whether the sky is
blue or grey.*

It is esoteric to the mortal mind that cannot understand,

this power from beyond the flesh, immortal and quite

grand.

I need no crystal ball for what my mind can envision

within,

I just need some closure to ease my nerves that's caused

my head to spin.

so, let me put this in simple terms, point blank, honest,

and strong,

I feel it all, so give it to me straight and tell me what is

wrong?

Love;

Your Son

The Mother

I really didn't know how I was going to tell him exactly what was going on, but I knew I had to. A lot of things were changing so fast and emotions were running high. I know how he can get. I saw what he went through when his father had a heart attack. He went on the attack and assaulted two inmates before being sent to the SHU where we could barely get ahold of him. I remember my husband Greg telling me that Jason does not need to hear any news of what's going on out here because prison is dangerous, and he needed to stay focused.

I know that he is in a dangerous world in there, and that makes this the hardest thing I've had to go through since telling him, while he sat in the SHU, that his father had been on life support for several weeks and we were going to go ahead and let him go. Boy what a destructive setoff that created! All the drugs and trouble he was in, I often wondered if he would ever get out. Well, he did, but not in one piece. In a few short weeks, he was back to doing the same things he had been doing of which lead him to eventually go on the run. I was living in Texas at the time, and to get him off the drugs and out of the street life, I told him to come out here where his sisters and I were doing pretty good, and so could he.

Well, he came out here only to find all the same kind of people that landed him right back in jail and returned to California. My memory may not be the greatest asset I possess, but things like this, I remember well. What I'm about to tell him is big news, and I don't know how he is going to react. I don't pray at all, but if there really is a God, please let him receive this well.

Dear Son;

There are so many things I must say to you before I
deliver some news,
first, let me apologize for my last letter that was not
meant to confuse.
Though my intentions were to tell you about all the
things that have happened over the past several days,
but it's all still so surreal, shocking, creating a haze.
A haze in my mind that covers like clouds that are hard
to except,
a dark brought rainy day with thunder, and I have not
slept.
How do I begin because I don't want you to worry or
lose control,
No matter what happens, I do not want you to lose sight
of your goal.
Because a mother only wants what is best, all for her
kids,
even if the pain comes suddenly buried deep in the ribs.
First, let me say for the first time in many years I am
proud of my only son,

I cannot stress that point enough even if my point over

and over was won.

Although I know this is not the end no matter the

outcome; whether good or bad,

and what I'm about to tell you is going to sting and

linger while making you real sad.

You have many questions in your mind searching and

seeking an honest answer,

there are tumors in my lung and bones and I'm sorry for

they are cancer.

With Love;

Mom.

The Son

It's the worst kind of news one can receive while locked up. The news that your mother or father might die. Prison life is already hard enough as it is without news like this making it that much more difficult. Almost immediately after reading this letter, I quickly ran to the phone.

There was a ringing. That long-lasting ring! Finally, I heard my mother's voice say hello. It took a few minutes or a few seconds rather for the recording to finish its instructions. Of course, my mother accepted the call and after a couple of seconds of small talk, I just had to ask what was going on.

"So, what the hell is going on?" I asked.

"Well," she began. "I went to the Dr. Because I just got my insurance. I've been having some pain in my chest. They did some x-rays and ran some tests. They found a lump in my lung, and another one also on my bone-my rib and its cancer."

This was probably the most devastating thing that I've heard in a long time. Just the thought of me losing my mother during this very important time in my life was extremely hard to imagine.

I started to remember back just 11 years ago while I was in the California State Prison in Solano. The news that I had received from my sister. My father was in the hospital on life support. He had been battling a severe case of pneumonia. They tried a couple of times to pull the breathing tube out of his throat to see if he could breathe on his own, but he couldn't. So, there he laid, in a coma. Once I talked to my mother. She told me that your father never wanted to be a vegetable. The fact that he had pride, maybe a little too much would stand in the way of a fight that he believed he could not win if that even makes any sense.

So I went ballistic! I went on an in-custody crime spree. Stabbings, beatings, drugs, drugs, and more drugs. The California prison system was a smorgasbord of criminal activity-never a dull moment. It all came to an end while in a day room I went on an assault rampage against two other inmates. The first dude ran, the next one caused a scene to the point of attracting the attention of the C/O but it didn't deter my attack; I made quick work of him. Pepper spray was flying, the sirens were sounding and before anybody knew what was going on, he was on the ground bleeding with me lit up with pepper spray; with my skin as orange as Donald Trump.

My mother remembers all of this. That is why she was so reluctant to tell me what was going on. She remembered how I sat in the SHU for several months and that she had called me finally one time to tell me that they were going to pull the plug on my father. All I really wanted was to at least say goodbye. It was arranged for me to talk to him or at least scream into his ear: wake up! Wake up!

I started to write a book about some really devastating stuff that happened to me when I was 14 years old, knowing I could never publish it while he was alive. He was the only one I could talk to about it since he was the last one left alive who knew all about it- being he knew the whole story and lived through it with me.

I never did get a chance to talk to my father. Prison staff was too busy eating, so they missed the phone call from my mother. Yes! She remembered all of that and everything else that transpired afterward. In the shuffle of moving from one unit to the next, mail had a way of floating around in limbo, often from one institution to the next. Finally, when I was released from the SHU, I got a letter in the mail from my now deceased father. It was like a letter from the grave. A letter giving me the green light to finally address all the trauma I had suffered, and a chance to fulfill his wishes of seeking out professional help in dealing with what I had bottled up for sixteen years of hell. It was an extremely difficult time in my life.

While you are incarcerated, the number one golden rule is to leave the outside world alone or else the outside world will rule you every single day and that is a recipe for disaster or death. My mother knew all too well what all of this looked like. After all, your family is incarcerated with you, so it won't take them too long to learn the ropes.

Of late, the goal is to convince my mother, that things were different-I was different! I mean why else were we doing this? This project that we embarked on was now several months along the way. In the beginning, it was very hard for my mother to believe me. I mean she heard it all before, seen it all before. The only thing that I always said, was I will do my best to not break laws no more. Although it can sound like a promise to the ears of a mother or father. It is never quite like that in the mind of the criminal child. This project of writing this poetry book together was a mother and son project-a way for us to finally bond. As time went on, and the more accomplishments I had under my belt, the walls my mother had built up had started to fall. Deep inside of her being, she has started to develop a knowing. It is all very esoteric, but it is an understanding that both me and her shared.

I believe she chose to break the news to me in this way because she knew that was the only way. Since we had been bonding through our ability-our gift! I mean, it did lessen the blow. I did not blow up into a rage, go on a rampage or get knocked off my square. And to her, that was the greatest blessing that she had received. It started to turn her into a real believer that her son was finally becoming a responsible human being. It was her ability to work magic. These poems were like spells, conjuring up good fruits of the labor involved. It's kind of like creating a vision board that I learned about in my pursuit of change. I often shared what I learned with my mother. You know it's funny. I've spent most of my adult life as an agnostic. You really had to basically drag god up out of heaven to prove to me that he was real. However, of late, I started to become very spiritual. I had studied many different theological topics for over 20 years. Knowledge gained from Masons, or Rosicrucians I had encountered over the years. While fighting this bank robbery charge in Oklahoma City, I had become deeply involved in studying the Bible without making a commitment to one religious denomination or the other. I started to find that everything that I have learned over the years had prepared me for a true spiritual awakening that would play a huge role in my change process and my mother was involved.

Being, that she was a confessed atheist, convincing her of any kind of presence of God was quite difficult. It wasn't my goal to convince her of the presence of God but to show her what the presence of God was really all about. It was not about religion, or commandments, or any carved manmade deities, churches, or temples, but about the ability of participation that we had within ourselves all along. An ability to create like a god does, an ability to manifest all our dreams while using one simple word as our foundation; faith.

This was the only way that I could convince her of the divine presence through action-my actions! And now that cancer was a reality of the struggle, things were starting to become a whole lot more real. It was a shock that this would happen, of course, nobody can anticipate the arrival of cancer and factor that into your plans for the future. This was a bridge that we were going to cross one way or the other. I believe wholeheartedly that she was in a fight to the bitter end. I mean it was in her nature. This was a woman who had experienced one failure in life after another. She never believed that she was the best mother that she could be. She felt her children did not turn out the way she wanted them to, that she somehow was responsible for that. Yet she never developed a pessimistic view of the world. She always maintained a strong level of optimism, for the most part, avoiding negative thinking and use to always get on me for it.

So, her magic was working, I started to develop a strong sense of optimism within myself. As our poetry tour went on through these letters, there was a turn into a much sadder and bleak area. Even though the content seemed to have been positive, you'll start to see behind the scenes they were very much different.

The Mother

I know this must sound selfish, but what a relief that was to tell him. It was like a huge weight was lifted off my shoulders. Surprisingly, he took it quite well. It was everything I hoped for in his response. Although I had no idea what was happening to him once the phone hung up and that is why I am working hard with him in writing this, to take both our minds off the situation. Plus, I been dabbling with the thought of getting this published. I know he would see it the same way. Imagine sharing this experience with others going through this exact same thing? That's going to be one of my last wishes if the worst comes. Publish this book.

I had to send my last note in after the poem because it would not have made much sense. Oh well! At least it got done. I will be starting cancer treatments soon, chemo, along with a pep scan to see how everything is going. I told him I'm going to beat this cancer. I'm going to beat it, so he does not need to worry.

I explained everything to him on the phone. I had to let him know in full detail what was going on and the worst-case scenario. I did not hold anything back. I could hear his tone of voice grow weak but stay strong without breaking into tears of which would have made me cry as well. The true test of his strength is going to come in these months ahead. For both of us, because I don't honestly know how I'm going to respond to the Cancer treatments, I have a low pain threshold.

Dear Mom;

The news you told me today on the phone,

made my heart sink in a river of sorrow like a small

tossed stone.

I promised you I would not cry,

I promised you I would hold my head of high.

Despite the fact, I'm in this cage,

your loving support stills my mind of rage.

Now my soul has a chance to overcome and grow,

to achieve all my goals my strength will show.

But my heart can't help but the feel this way,

with the thought that you'll be gone someday.

For Cancer struck your lung and bone,

this is what you told me on the phone.

If I could give your mine to save your life,

I would tell the surgeon to grab his knife.

Cut me open, take what you need,

because you're my mother, for you I'll bleed.

This whole experience has been my faith's test,

at least you're here right now, so yes, I'm still blessed.

Love;

Your Son.

Dear Son;

Your strength can weather all the hurt in life that you've
been through,
this is just a stop all over before you start anew.
Something called to your soul, so get your heart free
rein,
and follow where it wants to go to wash away the pain.
Your yesterdays will fall away to just faint memories,
if you let the faith you found color all it sees.
You know someday that I'll be gone, but my spirit will be
there,
to walk beside your every step and know that I still care.
My faith and love has always been there for you to see,
and through the years I've always known the man that
you could be.
So though the road you choose may at times be hard;
remember what I said,
and let what's past be the past just look ahead instead.

With love;

Mom.

The Son

After reading her letter, I knew that I would never physically see her again. It's that strange intuition that we have built inside of us. It's a knowing. I meant every word of what I said, I would most definitely allow them to take my internal organs to save someone who is as special to me is my mother.

For several weeks, I moped around the prison; a dangerous practice. You cannot allow the streets to affect you in any way shape or form. Just the fact that you were aloof when somebody could bring great harm to your life is enough to always stay on your toes.

My mother knew this all too well, as I explain this before. She knew what went on in here. But what was she really feeling? I mean here, on one hand, she's telling me that she's gonna beat it! But the way she describes it, I have some serious doubts. I mean my father died, it came all of a sudden. But can I sit back and watch my mother die slowly-or rather, listen to her die slowly? I was not prepared for this at all. Never once did this cross my mind.

So, I imagined what was going on in my mother's mind. All the emotions. All the feelings. Counting your days down until it's your last. Was she willing to fight this? I could picture what she was thinking. I was willing to bet that she was in straight denial. She started to go on and on about what she was doing differently. That she was not going to smoke any more. How she was going to start exercising and eating right. I knew it wasn't gonna happen. I mean come on! My mother had been smoking for 50 years! You can't just one day wake up and say I'm done. But that was her, always an optimist in a lot of ways, but deep down, she had a lot of pessimism with her as well.

So I could imagine, all the best intentions she had followed by a whole bunch of dreams and ideas that would not materialize. That's just the way it was in our family.

I woke up the next morning just like any other morning-early, Very early. I had an early morning ritual that I did routinely. It was called the lesser banishing ritual of the pentagram, followed by the banishing ritual of the hexagram. I would then stretch and run through my regular Hatha yoga sun salutations. My cellmate at the time did not quite understand what I did, but he respected it and never cast negative energy my way while I was engaged in what I was doing. But that would all change when my new cellie arrived. I knew I was gonna get a real piece of work as a cellie because most of these dudes doing time these days had no idea what it meant to be a convict. I knew all too well what it meant to be a convict, and I knew all too well what I was capable of. But I cannot do that, I couldn't risk tricking off my time. I had already made a secret peace pact with myself. I would do everything in my power to avoid violence. That would prove to be quite difficult. Reason being, I ran with one of the most notorious cars there was in the United States prison system. Whether it was State or Federal, everybody knew what a Sureno was, and a Sureno was feared and respected.

However, we were only human, capable of making mistakes with each other. That's where the real danger lied. I learned that lesson the hard way. I believed that I could talk my way out of any situation, that I didn't have to resort to violence. But it backfired against me one day with one of my own. The physical hurt was nothing, the mental hurt was the worst. There was a moment when I lost control of my rational thinking. Everything that I was going through with my mother including all the promises I was making was about to be severely challenged.

Basically, what I'm trying to say is, that I was gonna kill somebody for what I felt was humiliation and disrespect. I remember sitting in my cell with my homie Dopey telling him about what happened. Describing everything to him in full detail. I knew that the homie packed hard candy (Knife). I was asking him if he could part with his knife knowing he had others buried all over the compound. What happened next was shocking. Dopey refused! Somebody like him would never refuse something like that. Honor and respect was a big deal for all of us, and when you were just disrespected, you handled your business. So why would he refuse? I believed there were powers within us that we couldn't understand. As a result, there are moments when these powers save us from our own irrational decision making before it's too late. Dopey was obviously driven by some unseen power to prevent me from making a huge mistake. Reason being, that would have been my life, and I would not be sitting here writing this book right now. My life would have been over. Being that I am in my forties now, I could imagine that I would not survive another 20 or 30 years in prison for murder. Let me just go ahead and swallowed my pride and walk away while keeping my life from being destroyed beyond repair.

All of this made me think. I went into a deep-thinking process, one that allowed me to make some hard choices. Thus far, I had been kind of halfway in and halfway out. The whole experience that I just went through, now add on what I'm going through with my mother, allowed me to fully commit to the peace process. This would not be easy, but it was gonna be done. I would suffer a lot of ridicule, but it was going to be done.

So I promised that I was gonna be strong. That I was gonna push on no matter what. I was gonna walk out of this prison in one piece and in peace. With all that in mind, I was prepared for my next letter. My mother would read everything I just wrote right now. I fully understand what I put her through and the one thing that I can guarantee is, I promise to be strong and not blow my time.

The Mother

So, I have a confession. One that's strange, because I know he's going to read this once it's sent out. I am fighting for my life through chemotherapy and all the other treatment that is horrible beyond belief. My hair is falling out, and my youngest daughter Jeanette bought me a beanie to cover my now bald head. I looked in the mirror and was heartbroken at what I saw; a once beautiful woman with long black hair, briefly blonde, reduced to the image of a hag. This in itself was enough for me to wanna give up. How could I not look at myself and cry? I don't know if Jeanette would care how I felt, but I started to think back on my life and reflect on what kind of a mother I was to my children. Jeanette feels I was a horrible mother, my eldest Julie thought I did alright. I knew I had to ask Jason what he believed. I never really gave much thought to his opinion since he has spent most of his adult life in prison, so I often forget just how much he has missed.

As far as how Jeanette feels, it hurts to know that I failed her and lost her respect, who knows how long ago. I know I failed to protect her from abuses she told me about. I know I've overstepped my boundaries in the her parenting of her kids. But I at least want her to know that no matter what, she is my baby girl and I love her very much.

Part of me wanted to give up. It's the guilt I feel for everything that has gone wrong in the lives of my children. As I sit here on this patio chair I can't help but look into the ashtray on the counter. Yes, I'm still smoking despite the treatment. Yes, I know it is hurting them knowing that I am doing it. So now you know Jason, I'm still smoking. But somehow, I think you already knew, didn't you? For the first time in all of this, my son's hardheadedness made sense. He got it from me and my side of the family.

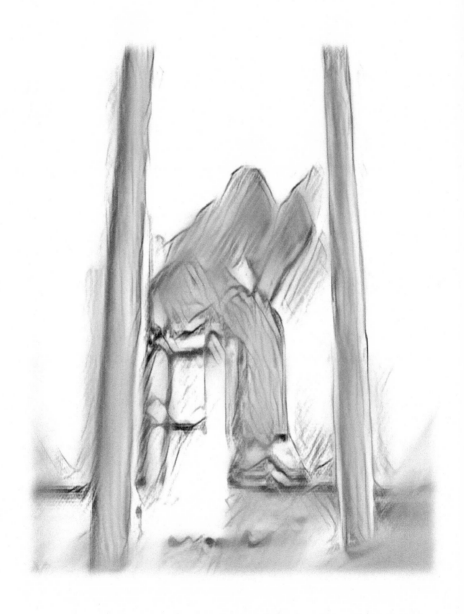

Dear Mom;

I promise you I will be strong,

I promise you I will discern, right from wrong.

It has never been clearer until today,

that everything I had done, on your heart it did weigh.

That I ran the streets with a total lack of control,

not like the son you wanted me to be, one with a positive

goal.

But instead, you watched a young boy grow into a thug,

never knowing when you would receive that final hug.

I made you worry, waiting by the phone,

oh, how that fear must have chilled your every bone.

Selfish was I for not understanding a mother's pain,

how my destruction depleted your life, like water down

the drain.

I know I can't take back everything that I had done,

all those times away from sanity that I had run.

But please hold on, for you will see,

that I will finally become that man that you knew I could

be.

Love;

Your Son.

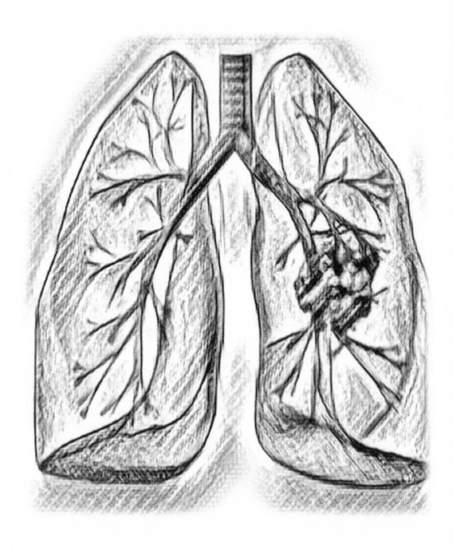

Dear Son;

All I ever wanted was for you to demonstrate the true
strength you always had,
for you to look at all the good that you possessed instead
of all the bad.
Please do not let your strength rest or stand on me
alone,
be humble in all that you face through this world with a
heart of stone.
Because you are my only son you have always been my
little boy,
when I consider your eyes of blue I see a child and his
toy.
That is how a mother sees her child from birth into a
man,
wishing all the best for much success; happiness the
master plan.
But when trouble comes, and darkness looms I stand
right by your side,
for a mother's love is unconditional it cannot run and
hide.
I will hold on for as long as I can until you are set free,

but even if I'm gone from this life I want you to agree.

That you will swallow your pride and face challenges, no matter what it brings,

fly like a bird in this life for freedom spreads its wings.

And when you have stayed the course remember where you been,

that is what you will need to do when the worse hits you on the chin.

With love;

Mom.

The Son

I can't even describe to you just exactly what was going on inside of me. I remembered back to all those times I spent as a street thug with no direction. With not a care in the world if I died or who I was hurting. When you are on the streets, the same as in prison, you do not occupy your mind with such matters. Once you have had time to clear your head, life becomes much easier.

Now here I am in a moment of great torment and emotion. How can I cope with all of this that is going on inside of me? As of today, I have learned plenty of tools to assist me in this journey. Coping skills, I never possessed before. Throughout the 20 plus years of incarceration, I never took any kind of program to help me out of the rut I was in. I gotta say, this one is so intense that you either bend, break, or stand strong.

Without sounding like a salesman, I highly recommend this kind of treatment to everyone doing time. If you are serious about changing and moving forward with your life you can do it and be successful at it. For anyone hearing this please understand that I am you. And for you mommas out there hearing this, my mother, Linda Is you. With that being said, the two of you, mother and child, can create a bond and weather this experience, maybe not with ease, but with love and open-mindedness.

We learn that it is cognitive-emotive dissonance that keeps us trapped in the departure from rational thought. But it is a willingness that fuels us. I understand a mother's pain now. I can hear her every word like never before. Just like a true parent, she refused to allow me to rest all on her alone.

"Please do not let your strength rest or stand on me alone; Be humble in all that you face through this world with a heart of stone."

Be strong, child. Do not allow this trial to be your undoing. Build strength from it and move forward no matter what the outcome is. "But when trouble comes, and darkness looms I stand right by your side; For a mother's love is unconditional for it cannot run and hide." And that is what it is. Her spirit will remain forever in my life. no matter what the struggle may be, she is there. No matter how high the obstacle is, she is there.

For her to hold on as long as she could was the best I could hope for. But I knew the cancer was deeper than she said it was. I found out through my sister just how bad it was. They had moved my mother to hospice care since the cancer was now spreading to other parts of her body. It moved from the bone and started to penetrate other parts of her body namely her brain. I started to notice changes in her when she would not answer her phone for my calls. There were times she did answer and I heard her voice pick up and say hello. Instead of excepting the call, she would hang up. Next thing I knew I was talking to my brother Steve who told me that she was getting confused and said that "Jason came by to visit me today" Steve had to remind her that I was still in Prison. She would look perplexed than say "Oh Yeah. Oh yeah. Why is he there again?"

Then her memory was jarred back to life with my next letter. Just like that, we resumed the conversation at best one last time.

The Mother

I'm sorry, it is getting extremely difficult to maintain my train of thought. There are giant time gaps in this book that I'm sorry for. I just did not have the strength or mental ability to put anything down on paper. Plus, I moved around a bit, started staying with Julie, my eldest Daughter for a while in a trailer park but that didn't work out as smooth as I would hope for. I just needed to take a break from living with Jeanette. I don't know why, but I felt like I was just becoming too much of a burden on her. We seemed to argue more than I liked.

I have been bouncing back and forth like a ball since Greg died, no longer having a home of my own. I think it's no secret at this point that I know I don't have much life left in me. I am in hospice now, no longer a burden on my children. Jeanette sometimes comes by to see me, and we've gone to play bingo a couple of times. Steve spends a lot of time with me of which is great. Over the years he has always called me mom, and over the years I may never have told him this, but I love him like he is my own son.

Has he taken Jason's place as my son? No, but he has been here over the years and I am thankful for that. There were times that I hoped Steve would rub off on Jason in the few short times he was here. But Jason does what Jason does and that is all I can really say about that. I tell Steve how proud I am of Jason these days. He doesn't roll his eyes or argue the point with me, he just says yeah that's great Mom, hopefully, he has learned a lesson and does good. I know he will. I know he will. And I Finally had a chance to tell him that he needs to publish our book. Without any hesitation, he said yes. My son, The best-selling author. That is what I envisioned for him.

Our last conversation on the phone was the best one in a long time. I finally got to ask him what kind of a mother I was, and do you know what he said?

"Mom I want you to know that it isn't your fault for how I turned out. You are a great mother, and I have always loved you and I am sorry I never made you proud. But the one thing I do know is my choices were mine alone to make, and they had nothing to do with your parenting. You did the best job you could have done."

Tears welled up in my eyes as I told him thank you. The peace he gave me with those words prepared me for what was to come. I told him that he helped renew my faith in something powerful beyond this world. I felt it around me. I'm so proud of you Jason, I just want you to know that. I really had to say this before I was unable to.

Dear Mom;

Yes, life has hit me on the chin and knocked me on my

ass,

but I guess this is how one's taught, with experience the

class.

Good news! I graduated from this program that

sharpened up my skills,

I now see the error of my thoughts that brought me pain

and all the chills.

There are stages of change, and anger control to lead

the horse to water,

instead of this misguided irrational path, like a sheep to

the slaughter.

I know you are in hospice care, but you say it's not too

bad,

if I lacked what I learned this situation would make me

mad.

Lash out, hurt someone is how I use to cope,

but now I work to think things through and cling onto

this hope.

That you will last until I'm out, six months is not so far,

watch your little boy in action as he reaches for the

highest star.

I know you say you cannot wait, to see this all unfold,

but the news that I hear is bad and that is what I'm told.

Please let me hear it from you, confirm all that I hear,

is it time to say goodbye as the moment that I fear?

Love;

Your Son.

Dear Son;

Although at times I thought I was not the best mother I
could be,

there were even moments that cut you deep, at times I
refused to see.

I cried so many salty tears, and still, god would never
come,

I prayed with not a single call until I believed god was
dumb.

How could there be a god above who ignored a mother's
prayer?

How could he watch over all this grief as if he does not
care?

I know you have great faith in this father up above,

when I die and face him there I'll ask him where's his
love?

Honestly, I would rather stay a ghost like the wind upon
the land,

to be a presence in my child's life and hold onto his
hand.
This Cancer is running wild in my body from my lung
into my head,
yes, I think the secrets out that the Cancer it has spread.
Soon I will lose my thoughts and things I will forget,
so, let me say some things and set them straight in case
you might regret.
Your life turned the way it did for reasons we do not
know,
but if you do not appreciate what's taught, then your
spirit will never grow.
It does not matter now how I feel if your path had let me
down,
even if most of the time in life, you caused your mom to
frown.
I want this to sink in real deep, all the pain that you have
caused,
there were many sleepless nights I worried for you, my
breath stood still in pause.
Worried that I would receive that call that your life had
met its end,

or that you were in a cell where for life you would there

spend.

But now here you are, with a chance to let this all sink

in,

I say all this to you now, before my mind it starts to spin.

Don't let this lesson go away as something you forgot,

remember where you been so long, and never lose that

thought.

With Love;

Mom.

THE SON NOW GRIEVES

Within three weeks after her last poem, my mother was gone. It was amazing how she put that last poem together from a hospice bed. I never did get a chance to ask her how she did it. I figured they must have had a computer somewhere. Whatever the case, I knew I had so very little time left with her that I wasn't gonna waste it on unimportant questions. It was tough enough already to talk to her let along ask her questions she might have already forgotten the answers to. I still remember that last conversation we had before she was on her death bed. She stumped me with her last request that I could not refuse. "I'm proud of you," She began. "I can't say that enough. I want you to promise me that our book gets published. It needs to be heard. It needs to be heard, just like I needed to hear it, and you needed to hear it."

Like I said we never intended on publishing this book, but her last wish for me was to get it out there and published. I mean she was very serious about it. I promised her I would do that very thing. No matter how hard it was going to be, no matter how long it would take, it was going to be done.

I was called into the chapel by the chaplain to speak with her one last time. It was strange to hear her like that, all weak sounding and so fragile. Most of what she had said I didn't understand. But nevertheless, I knew I would never hear her voice again. I said my goodbyes and listened to her hand the phone back to my brother Steve. I heard her say; "that was my son," with a faint hint of pride.

She slipped away into a deep slumber and never woke up. My brother Steve was there to hold her hand since I was unable to get a furlough to go see her one last time. I did not cry once she was gone. I did all that for months leading up to it. What I did was stand strong and finally turn my back on all reservations I held into any kind of tie of criminal living I might have had. I even, at the time, deleted most of the music on my MP3 player that held any kind of gangsta message. I needed to escape from all of it. I even started to distance myself from the prison politics even further than before; all the way up to the danger zone point. I was teetering on what some might construe as being a dropout or turncoat. I was neither. I saw gang dropouts for what most of them were, not someone who was ready for change, but someone who was forced out because they fucked up either by getting in debt or making a bad call.

My situation was different. There was no criminal matter I was running away from, and I didn't fuck up and wreck my career. I just woke up a few years back and was done with the bullshit that had got me nowhere in life. I had put in all the work I was gonna put in.

I did all I was gonna do. Let the peewees handle that shit, I was ready to grow up is all it was. Whoever had any other thoughts, oh well.

As I started to distance myself, I told the man in charge what my plans were and to please not stand in the way of them. We agreed to a compromise, up to a certain point. I had to stay out of trouble and keep my nose clean from all hustle activity. I humbly agreed. Furthermore, I wasn't gonna be asked to do anything, except helping a homie out if he was getting rushed. I prayed that it would never come to that, but for the most part, I was left to my pursuit of a better life. The biggest promise of all came with a warning. DON'T COME BACK! For sure. Easy enough. No matter what lies ahead, I will push on like a true soldier.

I talked to my brother on the phone regarding my mother's body. She decided to donate herself to science so that at least her body could be useful in the advancement of medicine. She once said why waste it on rotting in some coffin somewhere, why not allow yourself to help others? So off to the research lab her remains went. I asked Steve if he knew where she was heading, and he said; "Colorado Springs."

I went silent!

I was in Florence Colorado, just 20 or so miles from there. Out of all the places in the world her body could have gone, it ended up right down the road from me. WOW! I remember her saying to me that she would always be around me. Maybe that was her spirit guiding her body from Texas to the state of Colorado. It was a reminder that she meant it. She would remain close by always. And with that news, I cried.

How could I hold back the tears? I could not start in with the promises. My brother stressed the fact that he was there as a stand-in for me in my mother's final days. I got the point he was trying to make. He wanted to believe in me, they all did. him, my sisters, nieces, and nephews. They all wanted to believe in me and believe what my mother was telling them, but I was gonna have to give them something. Show them something. For now, as expected, there were some walls built up around them. With time I know that they will see what she saw. A change in the boy who for so long destroyed himself.

Soon I was going to be released. I had nowhere to go but back to the state where the crime was committed. That was the law. I had no legal residence to release to, so I had to go back to the state of commitment. The months ahead were for sure to be the greatest test of my life. I am going to a state where I've never lived or visited outside of the bank I robbed in El Reno Oklahoma.

So be it! If Oklahoma was where I was going to go, then Oklahoma was where I am going to overcome all the odds. I'm leaving this place a changed man. Even if I fail, of which is not in my vocabulary; nor is it my self-fulfilling prophecy, I have forever changed as a man. Everything I did and overcame thus far wouldn't be for nothing. I know that I have made my mother proud. And I know that we are reunited in spirit because I can feel her presence all around me, and she will not let me fail.

The next morning after her passing, I stepped out into the unit. I walked over to the computer where my mother and I wrote all these poems and stayed in close contact when not talking on the phone. Normally I would see the notification that I got a new email. I would click on the icon and be taken to new messages. There I would see her name. Today was different. There was no new emails. My shoulders slumped down and my heart sunk once more. I felt so alone. I decided to write her a message and send it out anyways. I simply wrote: "Hi, mom. Just wanted to say I love you and miss you."

I sent it out and walked away from the computer. I would periodically check to see if I got a response, but a response never came. She was gone, and the hardest part of doing time was ahead in the few shorts months I had left. I sat down at the computer and wrote her one last message:

"I love you, Momma. Thank you for standing by my side on this last prison term. And thank you for staying in my life beyond the body."

NOVEMBER 2017

I was released on January 11, 2017, to the halfway house in Oklahoma City, Oklahoma. All I had was the shirt on my back, and roughly 38 dollars on a debit card the Bureau of Prisons gave me from my trust account of money I earned as an orderly. I was not nervous upon release like most people are. I had nothing to be nervous about. I knew that with a clear purpose, and the will to do right, everything would fall into place.

The Greyhound bus rolled south into Texas and past the town of Amarillo where I met several FBI agents, and local law enforcement for the bank robbery. I looked down on the town that changed my life for the better now. If I would have taken a different turn or chose to let the cops execute me right there on the spot, then my mother and I would not have written this book. The power above no matter how you see it plays an important role in all of our lives. The experiences we face, and the challenges we must overcome shape us into who we are for reasons that we should never question. I cannot explain why my life went in the direction that it did. All I can tell you is that where the outcome leads me is somewhat of a miracle if indeed miracles do happen.

My destiny has lead me to this place and brought me the fruits of my labor. I have succeeded in overcoming many of the odds that others fail to beat. I am living on my own with a career, good friends, my health, sober, and crime free. I once believed that I was institutionalized but then I learned that what I believed was false. It was a self-fulfilling prophecy I had finally overcome; finally dispelling it as myth and a cop-out.

There is no challenge too big, and goals can be reached if you meet them halfway and extend your hand instead of tucking your hands in your pockets expecting your goals to chase you. The payoffs for my hard work also include family and old friends who now make it a point to encourage me along the way while standing by me watching this miraculous accomplishment. I am a better person today then I was yesterday. I am my mother's son. She believed in me, so I believe in myself and that is one of the main keys to success. You must believe in yourself and never give up. I am living proof that you can spend over two decades going in and out of prison, and in the end, find happiness in your life as I have.

Let this book stand, not only as a journey but as a testament that I hope and pray will inspire you to also seek out the happiness that I have found.

Thank you for taking this journey with us.

Footsteps

Footsteps always echo with footsteps from the past,
they keep us moving forward, make memories that last.
All that came before us, that tread the same old road,
helped us stay the distance while lightening our load.
And if you listen closely their voices you will hear,
with quiet words of wisdom, don't live your life in fear.
Although there'll be days of pain, and nights that seem
too long,
the light of faith you have within will always keep you
strong.

Found out I have Lung cancer Jan. of this year...still
fighting :)

The End, But the Beginning

This is not the end, but the start of what's to come,

from running amok, living life like a bum.

This is not the end, but the beginning of what I will do,

obtain as many goals as I can, many successes to accrue.

This is not the end, but a journey along the straight

path,

proving I can stand strong against adversity, at failure I

laugh.

This is not the end, but the beginning of true freedom

within,

finally coming to terms with the meaning of sin.

This is not the end, but my story of life,

for I now wield the pen, instead of the knife.

This is not the end, but the beginning of endless

possibility,

there is nothing I cannot accomplish to reach tranquility.

Jason JD Rutherford

December 2017

ABOUT THE AUTHORS

Linda Lee Rutherford started writing poetry over 50 years ago. During the 1960s she wrote, Soldier Boy, and Lucifer as a reaction to the world around her. She was published several times in many online poetry guilds winning many first-place prizes for her contributions. While poetry was important to her, Linda loved to quilt. She created many different beautiful pieces for her family while donating many others to charitable organizations.

She passed away from Bone, and Lung Cancer on June 20, 2016. Linda donated her body to science as one last gift to the world: this time to medicine.

Jason JD Rutherford has been writing poetry, lyrics, and other areas of literature for 28 years. After spending over 20 years in and out of prison, he finally saw the error of his ways and put forth a lot of hard work to change for the better and strive towards helping others break the criminal cycle as a reentry specialist and life coach. In 2018, He established Stand For Something Life Inc., a Non-profit Organization in the fight for Common-sense justice and rehabilitation. He is the published author of An Imprisoned Mind, and has more books to come.

He currently lives in Oklahoma City where he is working on other literary projects and works as a line cook in a fine dining restaurant.

You can contact Jason JD Rutherford@

twitter@jd_rutherford

https://www.facebook.com/jajaru44

https://www.instagram.com/author_j.d.rutherford/

https://www.youtube.com/channel/UC-Cmh-

Cg9kynsqVCHqd_5gLA

Made in the USA
Coppell, TX
25 September 2020